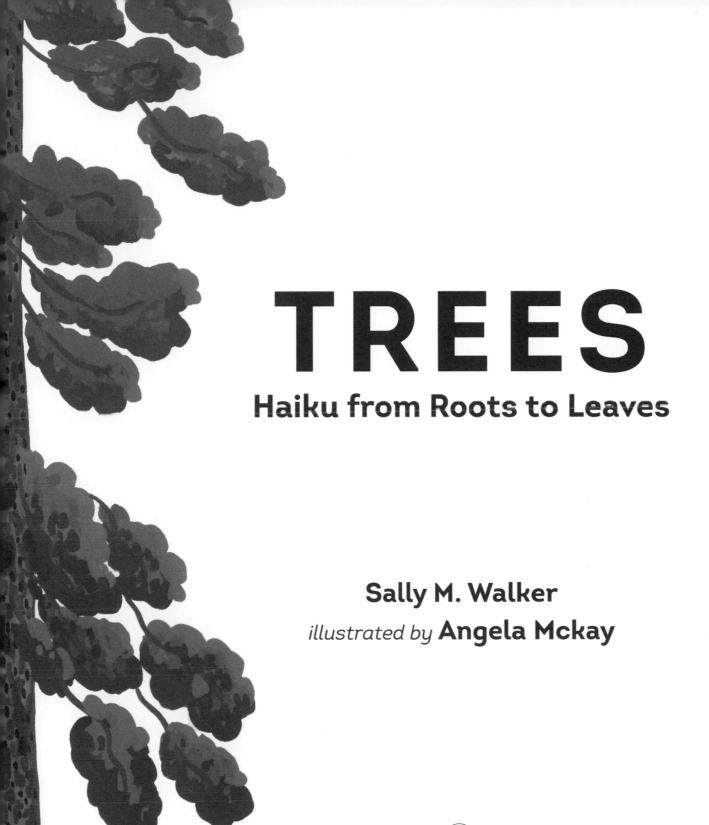

TREES

Haiku from Roots to Leaves

Sally M. Walker

illustrated by **Angela Mckay**

CANDLEWICK PRESS

IN TIMES LONG PAST

for millions of years
gargantuan tree ferns ruled
Earth's wet, warm forests

nudged by climate change
trees evolved survival tools:
wood, flowers, and seeds

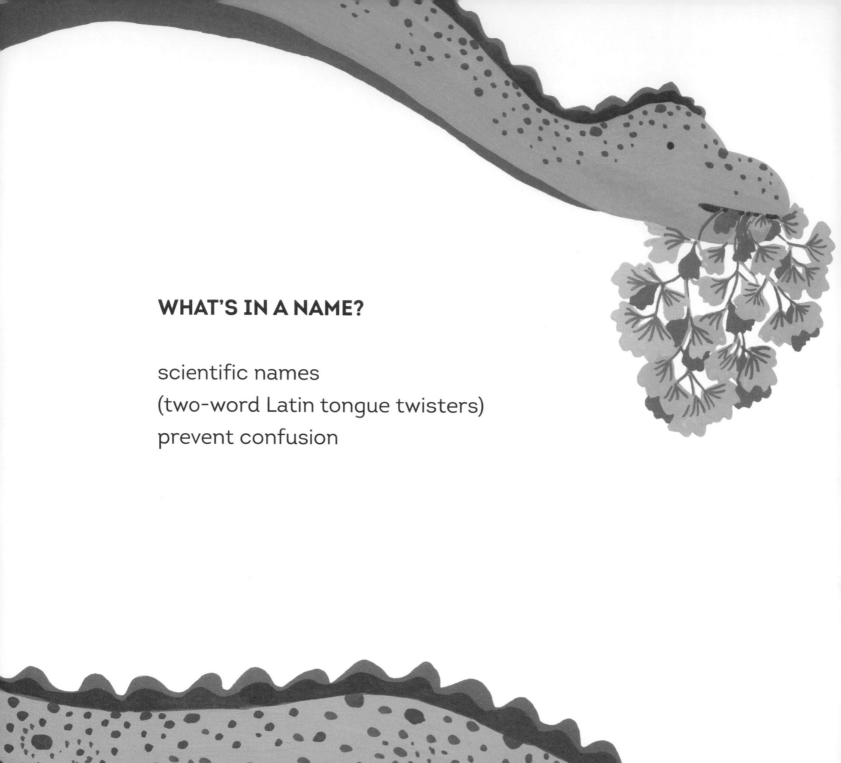

WHAT'S IN A NAME?

scientific names
(two-word Latin tongue twisters)
prevent confusion

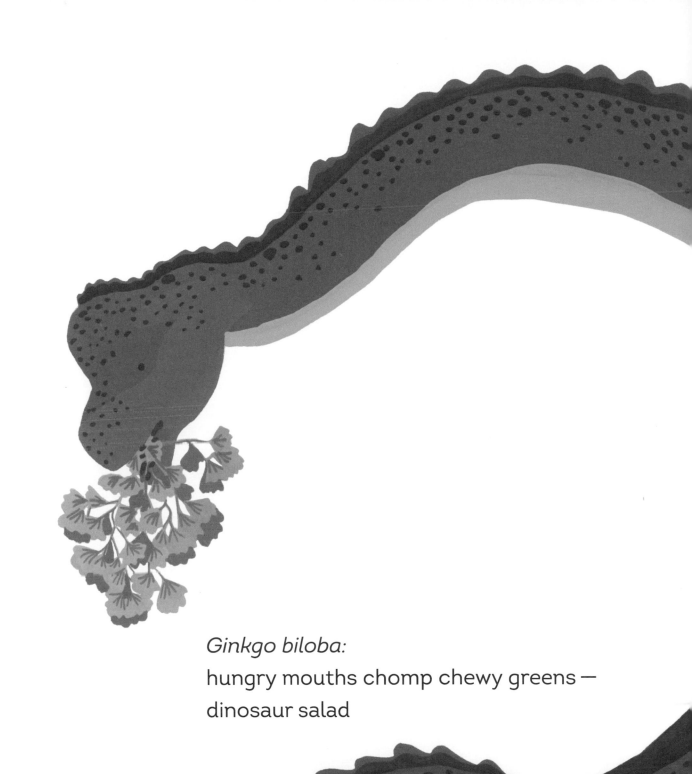

Ginkgo biloba:
hungry mouths chomp chewy greens —
dinosaur salad

SEEDS

crack! a seed hull splits!
a thin root tip emerges
and grabs hold of life

helicopter seeds
splash-land in a vernal pool—
startled tadpoles hide

covered with gray fur
pussywillow catkins cling:
kittens on slim twigs

porcupine-quill-sharp
chestnut burrs cloak tasty treats:
a squirrel eats lunch

ON THE OUTSIDE

widespread buried roots
joined to stalwart trunk joined to
widespread timber limbs

its bark age-furrowed,
the ancient bur oak cradles
Mama Robin's nest

PEEKING INSIDE

long, thin xylem tubes
zip water from roots to leaves:
tree elevators

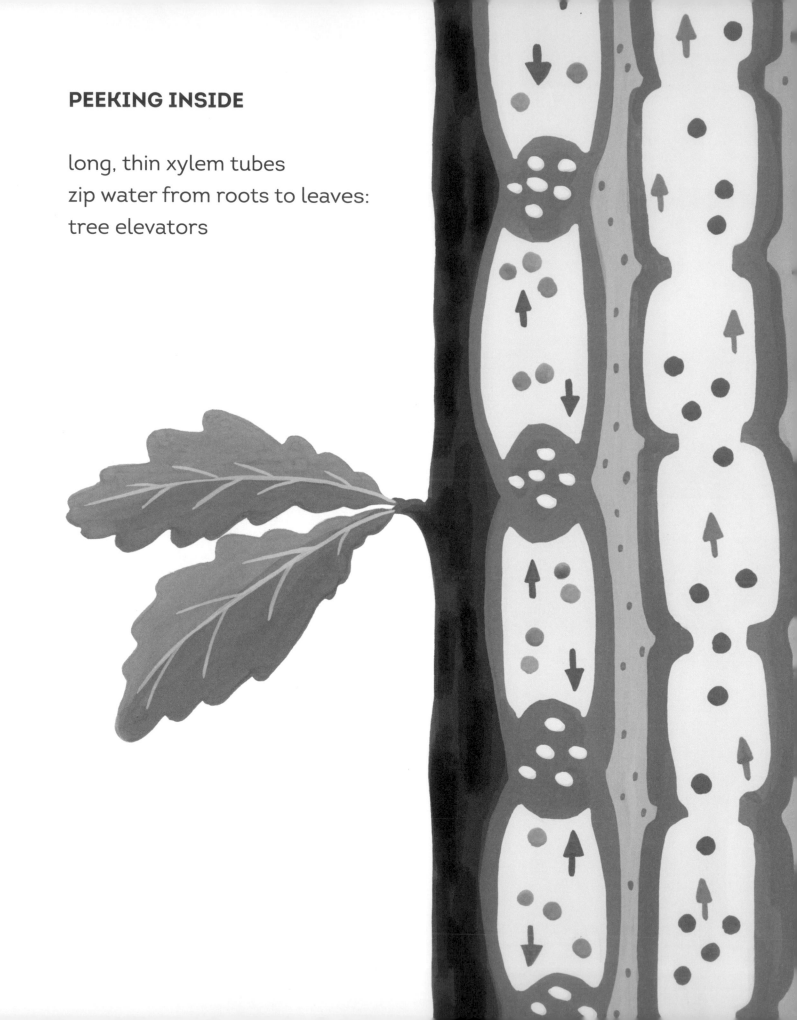

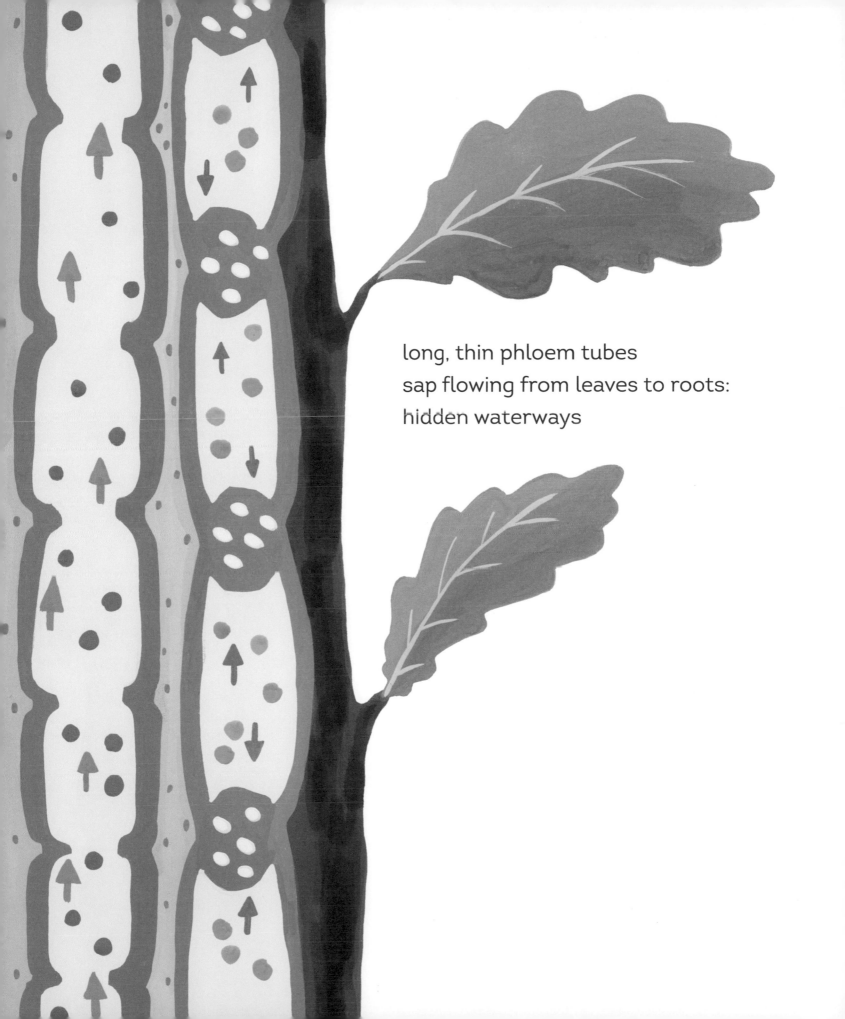

long, thin phloem tubes
sap flowing from leaves to roots:
hidden waterways

cold nights, warmer days
reawaken maple sap —
time for sweet syrup!

concentric circles
record spring and summer growth . . .
a tree's diary

TREETOPS

roller-coaster breeze . . .
flat-stemmed quaking aspen leaves
tremble as they ride

diamond-bright raindrops
sparkle on emerald blades —
jewels in an elm's crown

gray sky, heavy clouds . . .
a hemlock's waving branches
sweep snow toward the ground

winter storm warning!
frigid rain coats chilled needles:
green-striped icicles

LEAF LABORATORIES

energetic leaves
brew sunlight, gas, and water:
photosynthesis

carbon dioxide
enters open stomata
when the sun rises

stomata doorways
squeeze out surplus water when
they shut tight at night

farewell, chlorophyll . . .
brilliant reds and yellows sail —
avid windsurfers

their task completed
deciduous leaves let go . . .
a vibrant carpet

GOOD NEIGHBORS

vital oxygen
from stomata to our lungs:
trees are good neighbors!

airborne scent signals
roots sharing information . . .
trees communicate

WILD FORESTS

topsy-turvy sloths
in tropical canopies . . .
rain forest hammocks

thorny kapok — ouch!
playful monkeys prick their feet
climbing up your trunk

URBAN FORESTS

pavement, steel, and glass
surround trees in tamed places . . .
urban oases

hardy sycamores
shade sizzling concrete sidewalks,
cool burning bare feet

TIME LINE

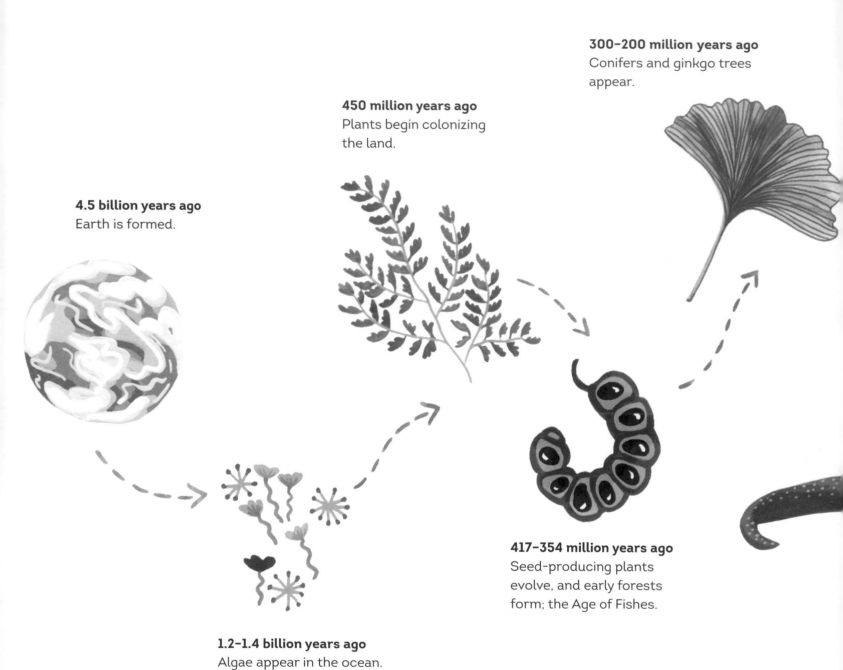

4.5 billion years ago
Earth is formed.

1.2–1.4 billion years ago
Algae appear in the ocean.

450 million years ago
Plants begin colonizing the land.

417–354 million years ago
Seed-producing plants evolve, and early forests form; the Age of Fishes.

300–200 million years ago
Conifers and ginkgo trees appear.

65 million years ago to present
The Age of Mammals

144–65 million years ago
Flowering plants evolve, and the first oaks, maples, willows, and other hard-wood trees appear.

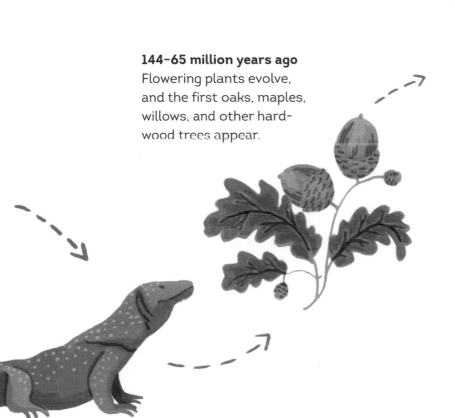

56 million years ago
Birch, beech, and ash trees begin to evolve and spread.

252–66 million years ago
The Age of Reptiles and Dinosaurs

In Times Long Past

About 400 million years ago, Earth's climate was much warmer than it is now. The air was damp, like a steamy jungle. Towering tree ferns, mosses, and plumy horsetails filled Earth's forests. None of today's trees existed. Over millions of years, Earth's climate got drier and cooler. Gradually the giant ferns, mosses, and horsetails disappeared. Other plants evolved in ways that helped them survive. Some developed wood cells. Tissue made of wood is strong and supports tall plants. Many wood-stemmed plants evolved flowers, fruits, and seeds as new ways to reproduce. More than 60,000 kinds of trees grow on Earth today.

What's in a Name?

A certain tree with large heart-shaped leaves may be called a cigar tree, an Indian bean tree, or the southern catalpa. So many names for the same tree—that's confusing! Scientists give every living organism a scientific name to avoid this confusion.

Scientists choose a tree's scientific name by examining its characteristics—its leaves, trunk, roots, flowers, and seeds. Trees with similar characteristics are classified, or grouped, together. This is called scientific classification.

A tree's scientific name has two parts. The first part of the name is the tree's genus. The second part indicates the tree's species. The southern catalpa tree's scientific name is *Catalpa bignonioides*. When scientists use this name, there is no confusion.

Ginkgoes are deciduous trees, meaning they bear seeds and lose their leaves in the fall. Many kinds of ginkgoes flourished during dinosaur times. But only one kind of ginkgo exists today. Scientists named it *Ginkgo biloba*.

Seeds

Many of Earth's early land plants reproduced by making spores. A spore is a tiny reproductive cell that can grow into a new plant. Spores need a ready supply of water to grow. Trees developed flowers as a way to become less dependent on an immediate supply of water. Flowers produce male reproductive cells called pollen. Flowers also produce

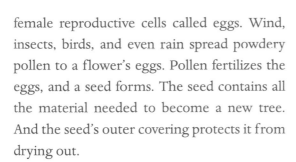

female reproductive cells called eggs. Wind, insects, birds, and even rain spread powdery pollen to a flower's eggs. Pollen fertilizes the eggs, and a seed forms. The seed contains all the material needed to become a new tree. And the seed's outer covering protects it from drying out.

When a seed has food, water, and a place to settle, it germinates, or grows. A tiny root tip and the edge of a baby leaf poke through the seed's outer covering. They are the first visible signs that important tree parts are growing.

On the Outside

A tree has three main parts: the roots, a main stem, and branches with leaves. Thick roots close to the main stem anchor the tree. Growing roots twist through the soil and burrow many feet away from the main stem. Some roots grow very deep, but most grow within the top eighteen inches of soil. The farther from the stem they grow, the thinner they become. Eventually, roots form a vast network of millions of thin-as-hair rootlets. These thin roots absorb nutrients and minerals from the soil. A tree needs these to survive.

A tree's main stem is called the trunk. It surrounds a tree's internal tissues, much the way the trunk of your body encases your internal organs. A trunk is made of wood cells. New woody tissue is added to the trunk every year. This makes the tree's girth increase. A sturdy trunk withstands strong gusts of wind.

Branches and leaves are a tree's crowning glory. In fact, botanists call the parts of a tree that are above its lowest branch the tree's crown. Like your arms, branches are extensions of the trunk.

As a tree grows naturally, its branches develop a particular shape. A tree's overall shape varies according to species. For example, spruce trees are cone-shaped, oaks appear rounded, and weeping willows droop.

Peeking Inside

Bark is a tree's skin. Like your skin, it shields a tree's inner parts from injuries, pests, and diseases. It provides protection from extremely hot or cold weather, as well as excessive rain and drought.

Trees have two layers of bark. The outer layer is mostly old, dead cells and easily peels or flakes. It may be rough or smooth, depending on the species.

The inner layer of bark is called the phloem (FLOH-um). The phloem is made of tube-shaped vessels—like super-thin drinking straws. The phloem carries sap from a tree's leaves to the rest of a tree. Old and dying phloem cells eventually become part of the outer bark.

Beneath the phloem, there is a paper-thin layer of green cells. This layer extends throughout the inside of a tree, from its roots to its leaves. (Think of long underwear and how it fits beneath your clothes.) This layer is where a tree's new wood forms. Every year, new wood is added as a pair of concentric rings. Spring growth produces a thin, light-colored ring. Late summer growth adds a second ring, thicker and darker than the other.

Together, light and dark rings form one yearly growth ring. Every year, the newly added rings slightly enlarge the tree's girth.

More tube-shaped vessels lie beneath the green layer. This tissue is called the xylem (ZYE-lum). The xylem is like a one-way street that goes uphill. Like a giant wick that begins in a tree's roots, the xylem absorbs minerals and water from the soil and carries them up into the leaves.

The wood at the very center of a tree is called heartwood. Heartwood is old xylem that no longer transports water or nutrients. A tree's heartwood spine has the strength to hold up hundreds of pounds of branches.

Treetops

Leaves keep trees healthy. Over tens of millions of years, tree leaves have adapted, or changed, in ways that helped each tree—and its babies—survive. Catching sunlight is one of a leaf's most important jobs. Some species developed broad leaves to catch a lot of sunlight. But too much sunlight quickly evaporates the water inside broad leaves. The leaf can overheat, dry out, or even die. To slow evaporation, the margin, or edge, of some leaves developed lobes. Lobes are indentations along a leaf's margin. A lobe can be rounded or pointy. Water inside a lobed leaf has more places to move. And a lobed leaf waves more in a breeze. Both of these things help the leaf cool off. In places that have four seasons, most broad-leafed trees lose their leaves as winter approaches.

Broad leaves can be simple or compound.

Simple leaves have only one blade. The blade is a leaf's flat part. The blade of a simple leaf attaches to a twig with one stem. Its margin can be smooth. It can be serrated, with sharp teeth. And it can be lobed. Maple, oak, catalpa, ginkgo, sycamore, and sweetgum trees have simple leaves.

The blade of a compound leaf is divided into a number of smaller leaflets. Together, they form one compound leaf. The leaflets share the same stem. The base of the leaf stem is attached to a twig. A shagbark hickory leaf usually has five leaflets. A honey locust leaf can have fourteen to twenty-six leaflets.

The leaves of evergreen trees such as spruce, fir, and pines are called needles. They catch less sunlight than broad leaves. Evergreen trees don't shed their needles every year. Needles remain on the tree for three or four years. This lets them absorb sunlight for a longer period of time. In the winter, heavy snow slides off the needles, protecting them from breaking.

Leaves also have veins. Veins enable water and nutrients to move from one part of a leaf to another, the way blood moves within your body's veins. A leaf's veins move nutrients into and out of the leaf's stem. The pattern of the veins on a leaf depends on the tree's species. Veins in evergreen needles are parallel from the needle's base to its tip. The vein pattern in the leaves of oak, cherry, maple, and sweetgum trees looks like a net. A ginkgo leaf has veins that spread like a fan from the base of the leaf out to the leaf's margin.

Leaf Laboratories

A green leaf is a mini chemistry laboratory. Tiny organs inside a leaf's cells bustle with chemical activity. Some of the organs make a green pigment called chlorophyll. That's what gives the leaf its green color.

A leaf is also a mini kitchen. It combines three ingredients needed to make a tree's food. Just as sugar and flour are important ingredients when you make cookies, chlorophyll is one of three ingredients that a leaf needs to make food.

The second ingredient is a gas called carbon dioxide. Each molecule of carbon dioxide contains one atom of carbon and two atoms of oxygen. Earth's atmosphere contains plenty of carbon dioxide. The underside of a leaf has hundreds of pinpoint-size holes called stomata. Stomata open during the day and absorb carbon dioxide. The carbon dioxide mixes with water already contained in the leaf. (The xylem carries the water into the leaf.) Stomata squeeze shut when the sun isn't shining.

While carbon dioxide and water are mixing, chlorophyll absorbs the third necessary ingredient: energy from sunlight. The energy that the leaf's cells absorb reacts with the carbon dioxide and water, causing photosynthesis to occur. Photosynthesis produces a sugar called glucose. Glucose is the tree's food.

The xylem carries more water and nutrients up to the leaves. They mix with the glucose. This makes a liquid called sap. (Maple syrup is made from the sap of sugar maple trees.) Each leaf has a network of veins, just as your fingers and hands have veins that circulate blood. Sap flows through a leaf's veins and into the leaf's stem. Then it flows into the phloem and is carried down to the rest of the tree.

When a leaf completes its job—making food—its chlorophyll breaks down and the leaf's green color fades. The pigments for red, yellow, and brown are no longer hidden by green. Deciduous trees manufacture food in a few months, during the spring and summer. By autumn, the leaves' work is done and they fall off the tree. Needles and evergreen leaves, like those on holly trees, last for several years before they complete their job and fall off.

Good Neighbors

In a way, people and trees are helpful neighbors. When we inhale, we breathe in oxygen. Our cells and tissues need it to make the energy that keeps us alive. Humans (and most animals) cannot survive without oxygen. When we exhale, we breathe out carbon dioxide. Trees need carbon dioxide to survive.

Leaves absorb carbon dioxide that people and animals exhale. They also absorb carbon dioxide produced by cars and factories when they burn gas, coal, and oil. Removing carbon dioxide purifies, or cleans, the air. Leaves only need half of the oxygen they absorb. Unneeded oxygen, plus any surplus water inside the leaf, seeps out when stomata squeeze closed. Then the leaf's unused oxygen is available for you to breathe in. Good neighbors, helping each other!

Wild Forests

A forest is an area where lots of trees grow and there are very few, if any, buildings. Earth has three main types of forests. Broadleaf forests grow in areas where temperatures change according to the season. Deer, foxes, raccoons, hawks (and in Australia, koalas) live in broadleaf forests. So do hundreds of insect species. Broadleaf forests include trees such as maples, oaks, ash, beeches, birches, and eucalyptus. Evergreen trees, such as holly, pines, cedar, and spruce, often grow among the broadleaf trees.

Rain forests are the second kind of forest. Rain forests have two seasons: a dry season and a wet one. Tropical rain forests—the humid, hot jungles where colorful birds, chattering monkeys, sloths, and poison-dart frogs live—grow near the equator. Annual rainfall ranges from 80 to 400 inches (203 to 1,016 centimeters). Trees grow quickly in the race to capture sunlight. The Amazon rain forest, in South America, is Earth's largest tropical rain forest. Kapok, banana, and rubber trees are a few of the many tree species that grow there.

Temperate rain forests grow along coastlines in Chile, New Zealand, Norway, and the United States, from Oregon to Alaska. They receive 60 to 200 inches (152 to 508 centimeters) of precipitation a year and have two distinct seasons: a long, wet winter season and a short, dry summer. The temperature in these rain forests ranges from −22 to 86°F (−30 to 30°C). Depending on the season, their precipitation can be rain or snow. A wide variety of animals, including wild cats, bears, elks, kookaburras, and opossums, live in temperate rain forests. Many deciduous trees grow in temperate rain forests. So do very large conifers, such as cypress, cedars, and sequoias (also called redwoods). Sequoias are rain forest giants. In California, one sequoia is 316 feet (96 meters) tall. Another has a diameter of almost 31½ feet (9.6 meters). Sequoias can live for almost three thousand years.

Conifer forests are Earth's third type of forest. The seeds of most of the trees in these forests form inside cones. Conifers include monkey puzzle, fir, pine, juniper, yew, and spruce trees. They thrive on hillsides in places where winter lasts several months. Deer, squirrels, rabbits, wolves, moose, and owls are some of the many animals that live in conifer forests. One conifer, the yew, has been useful as a source of medicine. Yew bark contains a substance that is helpful in treating certain types of breast cancer.

The roots in wild forests help prevent flooding by absorbing stormwater that could overwhelm streams and rivers. Roots hold the soil in place, which prevents landslides, erosion, and dust storms. Roots also filter, or remove, some pollutants from water as it seeps underground. Clean water is important for the environment and for safe drinking water.

Foresters are educated and trained to take care of trees. They plant seedlings, help restore areas that have been damaged by fire or industries such as coal mining, and offer advice on the preservation and conservation of mature trees. Foresters determine which areas of a forest are suitable for cutting as lumber and for other uses.

Urban Forests

Many people think of forests as wild, countryside places. But the trees city dwellers see outside their homes—in parks, gardens, their yards, and along the streets—make up urban forests.

City planners choose trees that invite people to visit parks—shady maples and oaks, evergreen spruce and pines. Streets lined with trees look welcoming. And hardy trees such as ginkgoes and sycamores are especially city-friendly because they can withstand pollution.

Urban forests are community assets. All the trees in the urban forest remove carbon dioxide and other pollutants from the air. They release oxygen, which is good for people and animals. Their roots capture rainwater the same way those in wild forests do.

Organisms that spread to new areas—often transported accidentally by people—are called invasive species. In the early twentieth century, a fungus from Asia arrived in North America and eventually killed more than four billion American chestnut trees. About thirty years later, another fungus, spread by bark beetles, devasted American elm trees. Shortly after 2000, emerald ash borers, a kind of beetle, arrived in the United States and killed millions of ash trees.

The fungi and beetles that attack American chestnut, American elm, and ash trees destroy xylem and phloem tissues. That stops the flow of nutrients. In a way, the trees starve to death. American chestnut, American elm, and ash trees used to line city streets. Their deaths left whole streets and large areas of parks with dead wooden skeletons.

Urban foresters have learned from these disasters. Now they suggest planting a variety of trees along city streets and in parks. If an invasive species (or any other tree disease) attacks city trees, a street or a park with different species will not lose all its trees.

It's great to plant young trees, but people should value old trees too. They have more leaves and add new wood more quickly than young trees. This offers more food and shelter for animals. An old tree's widespread, well-developed root system also absorbs more rainwater. Treasure, protect, and care for your city's "old-timers."

AUTHOR'S NOTE

Trees are one of Earth's treasures. From as early as I can remember, the songs made by wind-stirred leaves have been some of my favorite sounds. My sister and I imagined new worlds beneath two massive copper beech trees in our neighborhood. We climbed their ladder-like branches and became pirates, Robin Hood, or island castaways. Our father often reminded us that trees are good neighbors and to treat them well. The three baby white pine trees he planted in the backyard where we grew up are now sixty years old, and at least as many feet tall. Today, I love looking at the three white pines that I planted, ten years ago, in the yard of the home where I now live.

What trees grow where you live? Getting to know the trees that surround you is a great way to learn about nature. Look at spring buds. Compare summertime leaf shapes. When autumn arrives, jump in a pile of raked leaves.

Many cities and towns have outreach programs that teach people about the trees in their community. These programs suggest ways that individuals can help encourage the planting and protection of a community's trees. Ask an adult to phone or email your local government offices. Find out if someone there can help you learn more about the trees in your community. You'll be glad you did!

GLOSSARY

bark: a tree's wood outer covering

blade: the flat, broad surface of a leaf

botanists: scientists who study plants

bur: the prickly covering, or case, of a seed

canopy: one of the upper layers of leaves in a forest

carbon dioxide: a gas found in Earth's atmosphere

chlorophyll: a pigment that gives leaves a green color

fungus (pl. fungi): an organism that helps plant and animal remains decompose

margin: the outer edge of a leaf

oxygen: a gas found in Earth's atmosphere that is necessary for most animals

phloem: a network of cells and tubes that carries nutrients from a tree's leaves to its roots

photosynthesis: a tree's food-making process, which uses energy from sunlight and chlorophyll to convert water and carbon dioxide into a sugary food

pollen: the male reproductive cells produced by flowers

stomata: tiny holes on the underside of a leaf

vernal pool: a seasonal pool, often lined with fallen or dead leaves, that is a habitat for certain plants and animals (such as spring peepers)

xylem: a network of cells and tubes that carries nutrients from a tree's roots to its leaves

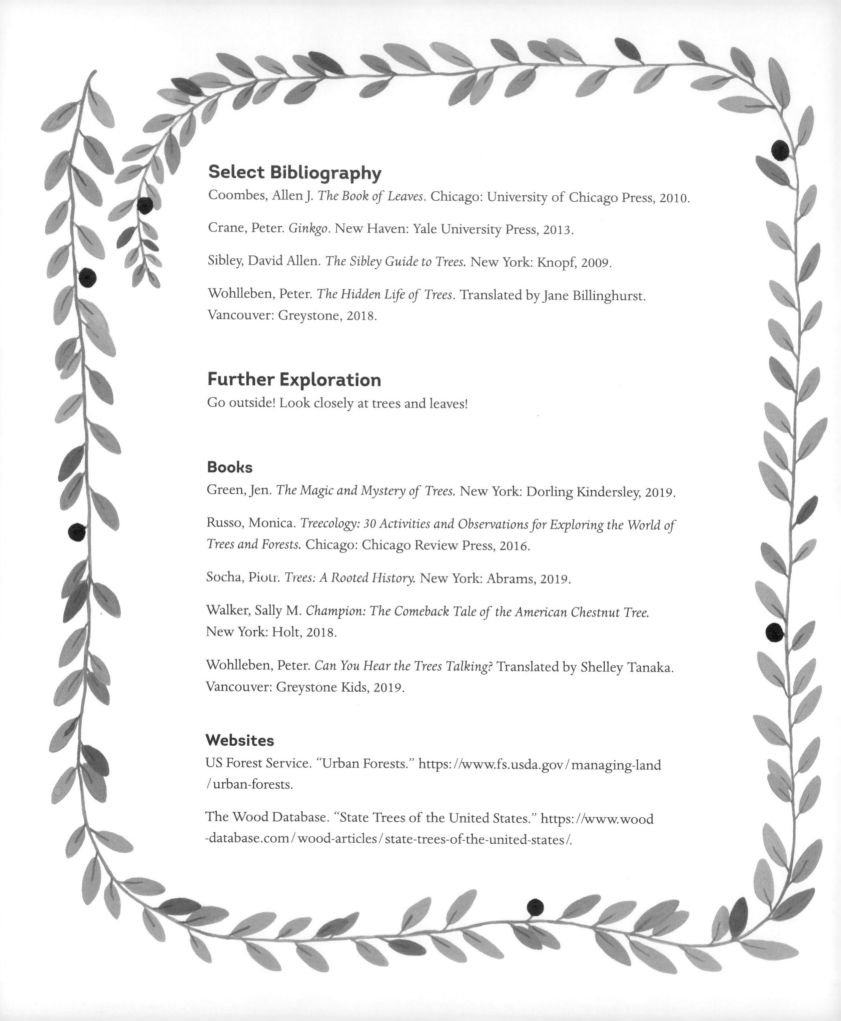

Select Bibliography

Coombes, Allen J. *The Book of Leaves*. Chicago: University of Chicago Press, 2010.

Crane, Peter. *Ginkgo*. New Haven: Yale University Press, 2013.

Sibley, David Allen. *The Sibley Guide to Trees*. New York: Knopf, 2009.

Wohlleben, Peter. *The Hidden Life of Trees*. Translated by Jane Billinghurst. Vancouver: Greystone, 2018.

Further Exploration

Go outside! Look closely at trees and leaves!

Books

Green, Jen. *The Magic and Mystery of Trees*. New York: Dorling Kindersley, 2019.

Russo, Monica. *Treecology: 30 Activities and Observations for Exploring the World of Trees and Forests*. Chicago: Chicago Review Press, 2016.

Socha, Piotr. *Trees: A Rooted History*. New York: Abrams, 2019.

Walker, Sally M. *Champion: The Comeback Tale of the American Chestnut Tree*. New York: Holt, 2018.

Wohlleben, Peter. *Can You Hear the Trees Talking?* Translated by Shelley Tanaka. Vancouver: Greystone Kids, 2019.

Websites

US Forest Service. "Urban Forests." https://www.fs.usda.gov/managing-land/urban-forests.

The Wood Database. "State Trees of the United States." https://www.wood-database.com/wood-articles/state-trees-of-the-united-states/.

For all who appreciate the wonder of trees, especially the folks
who are working to preserve, conserve, and restore them
SMW

For Tui and all the tree lovers of the next generation
AM

First edition 2023

Library of Congress Catalog Card Number 2022936943
ISBN 978-1-5362-1550-2

22 23 24 25 26 27 CCP 10 9 8 7 6 5 4 3 2 1

Printed in Shenzhen, Guangdong, China

This book was typeset in Intro.
The illustrations were done in gouache.

Candlewick Press
99 Dover Street
Somerville, Massachusetts 02144

www.candlewick.com